NAME:

- - - - - - - - - - - - - - - - - -

What

GOOD

WILL you do

TODAY?

WHAT do you Love MOST ABOUT this WORLD?

HOW ARE YOU going to use YOUR talents?

WHAT ARE you GRATEFUL FOR?

WHAT MAKES YOU feel REALLY ALIVE?

WHAT
DO YOU
DREAM

OF?

WHAT GIVES YOUR LIFE MEANING?

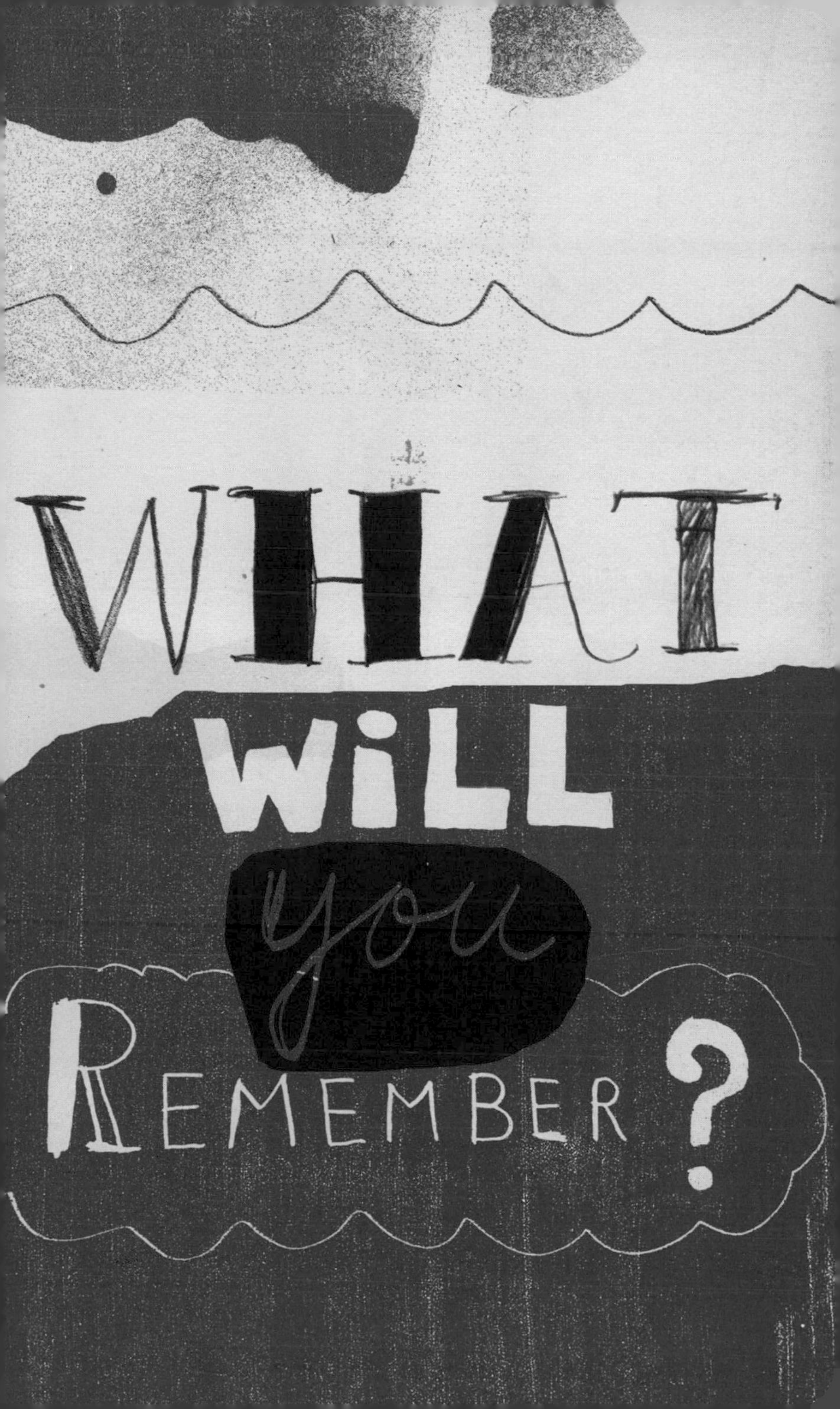
WHAT
WiLL
you
REMEMBER?